S0-DFG-558

The GRIBBLEGROT from Outer Space

A thunderous boom and a bright lightning bolt
Shook the whole house with a gigantic jolt.
Zoe leapt from her bed and looked in the yard,
Where a very strange creature had landed quite hard.

Dazed and confused, it stumbled around.
What could it be? What had Zoe found?
Zoe gave a gasp as over it fell.
It needed her help, that much she could tell.

Books didn't help Zoe, or give her a clue.
Where could she look? What could she do?
Somewhere, somehow, she hoped she would find
That the creature out there wasn't just in her mind.

UNSOLVED
Mysteries

YOUR PLACE
MY PLACE
SCIENCE ALIVE

7

Zoe, in despair and wanting to cry,
Said to the creature she thought it might die.
But just as she spoke, she suddenly saw
A red switch turned off right under its jaw.

ON OFF

She turned on the switch, and the creature awoke,
And these are the things it said when it spoke:
"You'll never find me anywhere in a book,
But come see my world – it's well worth a look."

"I'm a Gribblegrot," it said, then sped her away
Out into space, where they found time to play.
Zipping along, they flew far quite soon.
Why, before Zoe knew it, they'd reached the moon!

Whizzing along without a worry or care,
They zoomed past satellites spinning out there.
Ducking and diving, they were going so fast
That Venus and Mercury soon had been passed.

15

Warming her hands in front of the sun,
Zoe thought this to be the best kind of fun.
They flew away fast, then saw in the stars
A little, red ball that looked just like Mars.

Yelling and shouting and feeling quite sick,
From riding along on a comet so quick,
Zoe and the Gribblegrot wanted to land,
But out there in space, they had nowhere to stand.

Rushing ahead, they raced far into space.
The edge of the universe Zoe now faced!
With nothing ahead and so much behind,
Wherever she looked, there was nothing to find.

Surfing along on the Gribblegrot's back,
Zoe came to a star that was blacker than black.
Spinning and spiraling down, down, down, down,
Toward a black hole in which galaxies drown. . .

Twisting and turning, with a hiss and a roar,
Head over heels, Zoe fell more and more.
A bright lightning bolt, then a thunderous boom,
And Zoe woke up safe in her bed in her room.